You Are Mephibosheth

At The King's Table

Dedication

For my beloved wife, Zaily — my covenant partner in this life and the one who daily points me back to the kindness of the King. And for our children — our four beautiful daughters and our son — may you always know that the Father's table is wide enough for every generation. My prayer is that you will never doubt the King's kindness toward you.

Acknowledgments

First, I thank the Lord Jesus Christ, whose covenant kindness is the heartbeat of this book.

To my wife, Zaily — thank you for walking with me in grace and covenant love, for encouraging me in every step, and for reminding me daily of the King's kindness in our marriage and ministry.

To our children — our four daughters and our son — you inspire me to live faithfully and to hand down the testimony of covenant to the next generation. Each of you is a reminder of the Father's kindness, and I pray you will walk in His grace all your days.

To our church family and friends — thank you for your prayers and encouragement.

And to every reader: thank you for opening these pages with a hunger to know the King's kindness. My prayer is that you will take your seat at His table with joy.

"So Mephibosheth ate at David's table like one of the king's sons."

— 2 Samuel 9:11

All rights reserved. No part of this book may be reproduced in any form without written permission from the publisher, except brief quotations used in reviews or articles.

Copyright © 2025 by Cole Bradshaw Published by The FaithFull Marriage Publishing All rights reserved. No part of this book may be reproduced in any form without written permission from the publisher, except brief quotations used in reviews or articles. Scripture quotations, unless otherwise noted, are taken from the Holy Bible, New International Version®, NIV®. Copyright ©

Contents

Introduction
Chapter 1 – Covenant Cut in Blood
Chapter 2 – The Fall of Saul's House
Chapter 3 – The King Remembers
Chapter 4 – The King's Chariots
Chapter 5 – Face Down Before the King
Chapter 6 – Grace for Covenant's Sake
Chapter 7 – The Gospel in the Story
Chapter 8 – Covenant Living
Chapter 9 – Covenant Spares from Judgment
Conclusion – The King's Invitation
Scripture References
About the Author
Invitation & Resources

Introduction

The story of Mephibosheth in 2 Samuel 9 is more than history. It is the gospel in living color. A covenant cut in blood long before he was born secured his future. A king sought him, carried him out of barrenness, and seated him at the royal table. This book walks through that story step by step to show how the covenant between David and Jonathan foreshadows the greater covenant cut between the Father and the Son — and how, like Mephibosheth, we are invited in.

At every turn we will keep the focus where Scripture keeps it: not on our worthiness, but on covenant already made; not on techniques, but on grace; not on celebrity leaders, but on the presence of the King. May you see yourself in Mephibosheth, and may you hear the Father's kindness for Jesus' sake.

Chapter 1 – Covenant Cut in Blood

The Covenant Ritual

Before we can understand the story of Mephibosheth, we have to go back—back to a field where two young men stood, pledging their lives to one another. Their names were David and Jonathan.

Jonathan was the son of King Saul, heir to Israel's throne by birthright. David was the shepherd boy who had killed Goliath, the one God had secretly chosen to be king. In a world where politics and power often meant betrayal and bloodshed, these two men formed something radical: a covenant.

In the ancient world, a covenant wasn't just a handshake or a verbal promise. It was a binding, blood-sealed agreement. To "cut covenant" meant that blood was shed to confirm its seriousness. The Hebrew word for covenant (berith) carries this sense of cutting.

Picture it: Jonathan and David standing together. Jonathan removes his royal robe and places it on David. He takes off his sword, his bow, and his belt, and gives them to his friend (1 Samuel 18:3–4). In essence, Jonathan was saying: "All that I am, all that I own, and even my future inheritance—I give to you."

It was more than friendship. It was a vow of loyalty sealed in blood, even unto death. Jonathan, the rightful heir to Saul's throne, was surrendering his claim, recognizing God's hand on David, and binding himself to David in love.

Why This Matters

This wasn't just about David and Jonathan. This covenant would one day reach far beyond their lives. Years later, after Jonathan was gone, it was this covenant that moved David's heart to ask: "Is there still anyone who is left of the house of Saul, that I may show him kindness for Jonathan's sake?" (2 Samuel 9:1).

The kindness (hesed) David spoke of wasn't mere generosity. It was covenant loyalty — a love that endures because it has been sealed by blood.

The Gospel Foreshadowed

Here is where the gospel begins to shine through the shadows of this story: • Jonathan, the prince, laid down his robe and weapons for David. • In the same way, Jesus, the Son of God, laid aside His glory and took on our humanity. • Jonathan bound himself to David by covenant love. • Jesus bound Himself to the Father by covenant love, sealed in His own blood. • Just as Mephibosheth later received blessing because of the covenant between David and Jonathan, so we are invited to receive blessing because of the covenant between the Father and the Son.

The covenant between David and Jonathan is more than history. It is a mirror of eternity — a foreshadowing of the greater covenant cut in blood between God the Father and His Son. And because of that covenant, we who are broken, crippled, and hiding in fear, are welcomed to the King's table — not because of what we have done, but because of covenant already made.

Chapter 2 – The Fall of Saul's House

The Day of Disaster

The Philistines came hard against Israel at Mount Gilboa. Saul and Jonathan fell that day in battle (1 Samuel 31:1–6). The people fled in panic, and with their fall, the dynasty of Saul collapsed.

It was on this same day that Jonathan's son, Mephibosheth, only five years old, was caught in the chaos. His nurse picked him up to run for safety. In the panic she dropped him, and the boy's feet and ankles were crushed. From that day forward, he was crippled (2 Samuel 4:4). The tragedy wasn't just political — it was deeply personal.

Life in Lo-Debar

Mephibosheth grew up in hiding, in a place called Lo-Debar. The very name means "no pasture, no word, no thing." It was a barren place. No abundance. No inheritance. No future.

But he wasn't only hiding from David. He was also hiding from the Philistines. These enemies of Israel had slain his father and grandfather and would have gladly finished the work by erasing any survivor of Saul's house. As long as Mephibosheth lived, he was a target.

This is the picture of our condition apart from Christ. We are not only broken in ourselves and afraid of judgment, we are also pursued by enemies who want us destroyed. Sin, Satan, and death hunt us like predators (1 Peter 5:8).

The Covenant Still Stood

Mephibosheth was hopeless, crippled, and hunted. Yet even in Lo-Debar, something greater than his fear remained. The covenant still stood.

This is where the story begins to look like our own: • Like Mephibosheth, humanity has fallen with its head — Adam. • Like Mephibosheth, we carry brokenness in our bodies, our hearts, and our world. • Like Mephibosheth, we live in "Lo-Debar" — a barren world of no true pasture, no true word, no lasting inheritance. • Like Mephibosheth, we are pursued by an enemy who seeks to devour us before we ever reach safety. • And like Mephibosheth, we fear judgment, not realizing that covenant love is waiting for us.

It is the covenant between the Father and the Son, sealed at the cross in blood. And it is because of that covenant, not because of our strength, that the King comes looking for us.

Chapter 3 – The King Remembers

Not Pity, but Covenant

Years passed. David was firmly seated on Israel's throne, the kingdom secure and blessed. Yet in the stillness of his palace, one question stirred in his heart: "Is there still anyone left of the house of Saul, that I may show him kindness for Jonathan's sake?" (2 Samuel 9:1).

This wasn't random compassion. David wasn't in a charitable mood, looking for someone to help. His question was driven by covenant. He remembered the day he and Jonathan bound themselves together in blood. He remembered the vow: "Do not cut off your kindness from my family—ever." (1 Samuel 20:14–15). David's search wasn't about what Saul's descendants deserved. It was about honoring a covenant that could not be broken.

The Search for a Crippled Son

Word came from Ziba, a servant of Saul's household. Yes, there was still one living son of Jonathan. His name was Mephibosheth. But Ziba added a detail that would have ended the conversation for most kings: "He is crippled in both feet." (2 Samuel 9:3).

In the ancient world, a crippled man was considered useless. To many, this detail meant: "Forget him." But not David. Covenant doesn't measure worth by usefulness. Covenant love doesn't ask, "What can you do for me?" It asks, "Who do you belong to?"

The Gospel Foreshadowed

The Father was not scanning the earth looking for the strong, the gifted, or the righteous. He was remembering His covenant with His Son. Jesus prayed in John 17: "Father, I desire that they also whom You have given Me may be with Me where I am." That prayer was covenant talk. Just as David's kindness was for Jonathan's sake, the Father's mercy toward us is for Jesus' sake.

The King's Resolve

David didn't hesitate. "Where is he?" he asked. Not: "Is he worthy?" Not: "What can he offer?" Covenant had already answered those questions. The only question that mattered was: "Where is he?" And so the messengers were sent to Lo-Debar.

Chapter 4 – The King's Chariots

The messengers of David thundered into Lo-Debar. Dust rose on the horizon, and the sound of hooves and wheels broke the silence of the barren land. The people of that dry place looked up in fear — for when the king's men arrived, it was rarely for good news.

Inside a simple home sat Mephibosheth, Jonathan's son. Crippled in both feet, hiding in obscurity, living under the weight of shame and fear. He had learned long ago not to expect anything from the world. For years he had lived with one thought: "If David ever finds me, I am as good as dead. And if the Philistines find me first, I am just as surely dead." Surrounded on all sides, hunted by the enemies of his house and haunted by his own brokenness, Mephibosheth lived as a man marked for death.

And now, the king's chariots were at his door.

Fear of Judgment

When the messengers spoke his name, Mephibosheth's heart must have sunk. This was it. He was being taken to Jerusalem, the very throne room of the man his grandfather Saul had hunted for years. In his mind, there could only be one outcome: judgment.

And behind that fear of David was another: the Philistines. If David didn't destroy him, surely Israel's enemies would. To Mephibosheth, his life was surrounded by death, from within and without. This is the sinner's condition too. We fear God's judgment, and all the while we are pursued by the powers of darkness. We live in dread of both — yet the covenant overrides them both.

Helpless and Broken

Imagine it: a crippled man, unable to run, unable to resist, utterly dependent on the will of another. He had no bargaining power, no defense, no strength to offer. This is the picture of every sinner carried to the throne of God. We are helpless, broken, with nothing to offer — no excuses, no righteousness, no escape. Left to ourselves, we expect wrath.

The Gospel Foreshadowed

The messengers who carried Mephibosheth did not come to destroy him — they came to bring him to the king's kindness. In the same way, Christ has sent His people into the world to carry others to the throne of grace. Like David's men, we are not the saviors — we are the messengers (Romans 10:14–15).

The King's Invitation

Mephibosheth did not yet know it, but he was being brought not to judgment, but to mercy. The kindness of David was waiting for him, not because of who he was, but because of covenant already cut. The Father does the same with us. He calls us out of our barren hiding places and brings us into His presence — not to condemn us, but to show us kindness for Jesus' sake.

Chapter 5 – Face Down Before the King

The journey from Lo-Debar ended at the gates of Jerusalem. The chariots stopped at the palace. Mephibosheth was carried inside, every stone step echoing with his dread. The boy who had once been a prince now lay crippled, dragged into the throne room of the man he feared most. If David didn't kill him for being Saul's grandson, surely the Philistines would eventually find him and finish what they started at Gilboa. To Mephibosheth, there was no future — only death waiting on either side.

And now, standing before David, he collapsed in utter humility. Unable to kneel properly, his crippled body fell prostrate, face to the floor, broken at the king's feet.

The "Dead Dog"

When David called his name, Mephibosheth answered with words dripping in despair: "What is your servant, that you should notice a dead dog like me?" (2 Samuel 9:8). In that culture, calling oneself a "dead dog" meant utter worthlessness. He was saying, "I have nothing to give, nothing to offer, no reason to be spared." This is the heart-cry of the sinner before a holy God.

The Covenant's Power

David's answer did not come from pity or politics. It came from covenant: "Do not fear, for I will surely show you kindness for Jonathan's sake." (2 Samuel 9:7). The covenant cut years before now stretched across time to rescue Jonathan's crippled son. Judgment was replaced by kindness. Death was swallowed by loyalty. Fear was answered with mercy. Mephibosheth had two enemies pressing in — David as he feared, and the Philistines as he knew. But both were overruled by something greater: the covenant.

The Gospel Foreshadowed

We stand before the King guilty, broken, and afraid. We know the enemy stalks us, and our sin condemns us. We fall at His feet with nothing to offer but weakness. And yet, for the sake of His Son, the Father says: "Do not fear." "There is therefore now no condemnation for those who are in Christ Jesus." (Romans 8:1).

The Great Exchange

At that moment, Mephibosheth's life was transformed: from fear to fellowship, from judgment to kindness, from hunted to protected, from Lo-Debar to the King's table. And all of it happened not because of who he was, but because of who Jonathan was to David. So it is with us. We are seated with Christ not because of who we are, but because of who Jesus is to the Father.

Chapter 6 – Grace for Covenant's Sake

The Covenant's Reach

The king who should have killed him instead promised kindness. David continued: "I will restore to you all the land of your grandfather Saul, and you shall always eat at my table." (2 Samuel 9:7). Land restored. A place of honor secured. Not because of Mephibosheth's strength, worth, or works — but because of covenant love.

The Meaning of His Name

Even Mephibosheth's name tells the story. His name in Hebrew can be understood as "dispeller of shame" (from bosheth, meaning shame, dishonor, disgrace). But another rendering can mean "man of shame" or "from the mouth of shame" — a name soaked in brokenness and humiliation.

How fitting for a man crippled, forgotten, and hiding in Lo-Debar. His very identity was marked by shame.

But covenant changes names. In David's house, Mephibosheth was no longer "the crippled one from the house of shame." He was a son seated at the king's table. His identity shifted from shame to covenant honor.

And notice this: Mephibosheth was restored as an heir of his grandfather's land, but he never became king. His inheritance was real, his sonship was secure, but David remained the king. So it is with us. In Christ we are made heirs of God and co-heirs with Christ (Romans 8:17), but we do not become gods. We reign with Him, but never apart from Him. There is one King, one Lord, one God — and our eternal joy is not to take His place, but to dwell at His table as His beloved children.

The Gospel Foreshadowed — Our Identity

This is exactly what the covenant between the Father and the Son does for us. We come with names marked by sin, shame, and failure. The world, the flesh, and the enemy brand us with labels: worthless, broken, condemned. But covenant grace gives us a new identity.

In Christ, the Father calls us: • Children of God (John 1:12) — not by striving, but by new birth. • Chosen and beloved (Ephesians 1:4–6) — not after proving ourselves, but before the foundation of the world. • A royal priesthood (1 Peter 2:9) — not through rituals of men, but by the covenant sealed in Christ. • New creation (2 Corinthians 5:17) — not gradual improvement, but a transformation that begins the moment we are in Him. • Perfected forever by one sacrifice (Hebrews 10:14) — not through repeated offerings, but through the finished work of Jesus. • Seated with Christ in heavenly places (Ephesians 2:6) — not waiting for some future exaltation, but already secure in Him. • Heirs of God and co-heirs with Christ (Romans 8:17) — not earning inheritance, but freely receiving it because of covenant. • The righteousness of God (2 Corinthians 5:21) — not working toward worthiness, but clothed in His righteousness by faith.

Our Covenant Mission

Covenant identity always flows into covenant calling. Just as David sent his men into Lo-Debar to bring Mephibosheth before the king, so Christ sends us into the world to bring others to the Father.

"Go and make disciples of all nations, baptizing them… and teaching them." (Matthew 28:19–20). "You are a chosen people, a royal priesthood… that you may declare the praises of Him who called you out of darkness." (1 Peter 2:9).

Through the covenant cut in Christ's blood, every believer is a priest under the one Great High Priest (Hebrews 4:14). This means the authority to represent God to the world and bring the world to God is not reserved for a select few, but given to all who belong to Jesus. We are not just invited to the King's table; we are also commissioned to go back into the barren places and bring others out of Lo-Debar.

Chapter 7 – The Gospel in the Story

The Parallels Unfold

By now the story of Mephibosheth is no longer just history — it is a living picture of the gospel. Every detail points us to the greater covenant, already cut in blood:

• David = a picture of the Father, who remembers covenant and seeks to show kindness. • Jonathan = a picture of Christ, the covenant partner whose love secures blessing for others. • Mephibosheth = a picture of us, crippled by the fall, hiding in fear, marked by shame. • Lo-Debar = the barren world, "no pasture, no word, no inheritance." • The Philistines = the powers of darkness, pursuing us to destroy before the King can restore. • David's men = the Church, sent into the world to carry the broken to the King. • The King's table = adoption, fellowship, and eternal communion with God.

Covenant Confirmed by Death

Jonathan's death did not cancel the covenant; it confirmed David's obligation to it. Likewise, the new covenant was enacted through the death of Christ: "This cup is the new covenant in My blood" (Luke 22:20). Hebrews 9:16–17 explains that a will/testament takes effect at death — so Christ's death activates the covenant's blessings for all who are in Him.

Two Enemies, One Covenant

Mephibosheth thought he was surrounded by death — if David found him, judgment; if the Philistines found him, destruction. But covenant love overruled them both. So it is with us. The sinner fears God's wrath and feels hounded by darkness, yet the covenant between the Father and the Son silences both fears: "No condemnation" (Romans 8:1) and "delivered from the domain of darkness" (Colossians 1:13).

Identity Restored

Mephibosheth's name carried shame. His crippled body carried weakness. His hiding place carried barrenness. But covenant changed all three.

- His shame was not merely covered — it was taken away, replaced with dignity at the king's table. • His weakness was not merely tolerated — it was met with sustaining grace, where the King's kindness turned his brokenness into belonging. • His barrenness was not final — it was replaced with inheritance that could never be lost.

So it is with us in Christ. The covenant changes our name, restores our inheritance, and secures our seat at the table.

Sent Like David's Men

The story does not end with Mephibosheth. David's men who carried him from Lo-Debar stand as a picture of us. We are not saved only to sit — we are saved to be sent. The King has commissioned us to go back into the barren places and bring the crippled, the fearful, and the forgotten to His table (Matthew 28:19; 1 Peter 2:9).

The Gospel in One Sentence

Because of covenant already cut between the Father and the Son, we who were crippled by sin, hiding in fear, pursued by darkness, and marked by shame, are carried to the King's table to be called sons and daughters — and then sent out to bring others in.

Chapter 8 – Covenant Living

Daily at the Table

"So Mephibosheth lived in Jerusalem, for he ate always at the king's table. Now he was lame in both his feet." (2 Samuel 9:13). His condition never changed. He remained crippled. But the covenant guaranteed that his condition would never again define him. He wasn't "Mephibosheth the cripple." He was now "Mephibosheth the son at the king's table."

The covenant didn't remove his weakness, but it removed the shame attached to it. It turned his brokenness into a testimony of grace. Every meal was a reminder: "I am here because of covenant." So it is with us. Each time we come to the Lord's Table, we are reminded that we are here because of covenant. The bread and the cup declare: "This is the new covenant in My blood" (Luke 22:20). Communion is not just a ritual — it is our continual reminder that our seat is secured, not by our worthiness, but by Christ's blood.

Living in the Covenant

We still carry weakness in our mortal bodies. We still live in a world marked by sin and brokenness. Yet none of these define us anymore. Our identity is anchored in covenant. As Paul says, "When I am weak, then I am strong" (2 Corinthians 12:10). Weakness becomes the stage where covenant grace is displayed.

Security in Covenant

Mephibosheth's place was not a fragile privilege that could be lost with one wrong step. It was secured by covenant. David would not wake up one morning and say, "I've changed my mind." The covenant bound him to faithfulness. So it is with us. Our place at the Father's table is not fragile, hanging on our performance. It is secured by the covenant cut between the Father and the Son. "If we are faithless, He remains faithful — for He cannot deny Himself." (2 Timothy 2:13).

From the Table to the World

Covenant life is not only about sitting at the table; it is also about carrying the King's kindness to others. Just as David's men went into Lo-Debar to bring Mephibosheth in, so we are sent into the world to bring others out of barrenness and into fellowship with the Father. Our seat at the table becomes the launching point of our mission.

The Testimony of Grace

Every time Mephibosheth appeared at the king's table, his crippled feet were hidden beneath the feast. His weakness was real, but it was covered by the presence of the King and the abundance of the table. That's covenant living: our weakness covered by Christ's abundance, our shame removed by His love, our place secured by His blood.

Chapter 9 – Covenant Spares from Judgment

Years after Mephibosheth was brought to the king's table, another crisis shook the land. A famine spread through Israel, lasting three years. David sought the Lord, and the Lord revealed the cause: "It is on account of Saul and his bloodstained house; it is because he put the Gibeonites to death." (2 Samuel 21:1).

Justice had to be satisfied. The Gibeonites were given seven descendants of Saul to execute as judgment for his guilt. Among those put to death was a man named Mephibosheth — not Jonathan's son, but another of Saul's descendants (2 Samuel 21:8). Two men bore the same name. Both were heirs of Saul's broken line. One died under judgment. One lived under covenant.

The Covenant Difference

Why was Jonathan's son spared? Because covenant cannot be broken. "But the king spared Mephibosheth son of Jonathan, the son of Saul, because of the oath before the Lord between David and Jonathan son of Saul." (2 Samuel 21:7). It wasn't because he was better or innocent. He was spared because of covenant already cut.

No Generational Curse

The guilt of Saul fell on his household, and judgment swept through his line. But Jonathan's son Mephibosheth was untouchable, because the covenant secured his life.

So it is with us in Christ. Many live under fear of "generational curses," believing they are chained to the sins of their fathers. But the covenant in Christ silences that fear forever: "The son shall not bear the guilt of the father…" (Ezekiel 18:20). "Christ redeemed us from the curse of the law by becoming a curse for us." (Galatians 3:13). "There is therefore now no condemnation for those who are in Christ Jesus." (Romans 8:1). Covenant breaks the cycle. What others call a curse, the cross has already canceled.

The Gospel Foreshadowed

Two men with the same name: • One bore the weight of judgment. • One bore the blessing of covenant.

The difference was not their name, but their covenant. Both were called Mephibosheth — a name tied to shame. • Outside of covenant, the name remained a curse: "man of shame," condemned under judgment. • Inside of covenant, the name was redefined: "dispeller of shame," transformed into honor at the king's table.

This is what covenant does. It takes the same name, the same brokenness, the same family line, and draws a dividing line of grace. One outside remains in shame. One inside receives a new identity. So it is with us. Those outside of Christ remain under the old name — condemned, guilty, marked by shame. But those inside Christ are given a new name and a new identity: children of God, righteous, beloved (Revelation 2:17).

The Testimony of Covenant

Jonathan's son Mephibosheth never had to wonder if he was next. He was safe — not because of who he was, but because of covenant.

Believers never have to fear condemnation, curses, or generational judgment. We are safe — not because of who we are, but because of Christ. And we do not work our way into fellowship with the Father. The very moment we enter into the covenant already cut in Christ's blood, we are received as sons and daughters with full rights to dwell with Him (Galatians 4:7).

Covenant doesn't say, "Earn your place." Covenant says, "The place is already yours."

Conclusion – The King's Invitation

The story of Mephibosheth is more than history. It is the gospel in living color. A covenant cut in blood long before he was born secured his future. Though crippled and hiding in Lo-Debar, he was sought out by the king. Though he expected judgment, he was given mercy. Though he called himself a "dead dog," he was adopted as a son at the king's table. And though his lineage bore the weight of judgment, covenant spared him.

Every meal Mephibosheth ate at David's table was a reminder: "I am here because of covenant." So it is with us. Every time we take the bread and the cup, we declare: "I am here because of covenant." The table of communion points us forward to the ultimate feast: the Marriage Supper of the Lamb (Revelation 19:9).

The Father's Call

The covenant has already been cut. The blood of Jesus has sealed it. The Father is not waiting for you to earn a place at His table. He is asking one question: "Is there anyone… to whom I may show kindness for Jesus' sake?" That question echoes across eternity, and today it comes to you.

Just as David sent men to carry Mephibosheth out of Lo-Debar, so Christ has sent His Word and His Spirit to carry you out of fear, shame, and barrenness — and bring you to the Father.

You may think, "I am crippled. I am unworthy. I am a dead dog." But the Father's answer is clear: "Do not fear. I will show you kindness for Jesus' sake."

An Invitation to Respond

This is your invitation. Not from David, but from the greater King — God the Father Himself. He is inviting you to stop hiding, stop fearing, and come take your seat at His table.

• You do not need to fix yourself first. • You do not need to earn His love. • You do not need to work your way into sonship.

The covenant has already been cut. Christ has already died. The invitation is already open. All that remains is for you to accept it: "If you confess with your mouth, 'Jesus is Lord,' and believe in your heart that God raised Him from the dead, you will be saved." (Romans 10:9).

Prayer of Response

If your heart longs to take that seat today, you can respond with a prayer like this. Remember, this is not empty words, but a choice to leave Lo-Debar behind and to live at the King's table. Mephibosheth could have resisted and gone back to his former life — but covenant called him to dwell with the king. In the same way, Christ calls you to count the cost (Luke 14:28), surrender your life, and receive a new one.

Father, I come before You like Mephibosheth — crippled, broken, and unworthy. But I believe You have shown kindness to me for Jesus' sake. I confess with my mouth that Jesus is Lord, and I believe in my heart that You raised Him from the dead (Romans 10:9). Today I receive Your invitation to be Your son / daughter. I choose to leave behind my former life in Lo-Debar and take my place at Your table. I count the cost and I surrender all to You. Thank You for the covenant already cut in the blood of Jesus. Thank You for giving me a seat at Your table forever. I choose to rest in covenant love today. Amen.

By Cole Bradshaw

Published by The FaithFull Marriage Publishing

Scripture References

(All passages quoted or referenced are from the Holy Bible, New International Version (NIV), unless otherwise noted.)

• 1 Samuel 18:3–4 — Jonathan makes covenant with David. • 1 Samuel 20:14–15 — Jonathan asks David to show covenant kindness to his house. • 1 Samuel 31:1–6 — Saul and Jonathan fall at Gilboa. • 2 Samuel 4:4 — Mephibosheth is crippled in both feet. • 2 Samuel 9:1–13 — David shows kindness to Mephibosheth for Jonathan's sake. • 2 Samuel 21:1, 7–8 — Famine; Saul's bloodguilt; another Mephibosheth judged; Jonathan's son spared by covenant. • Psalm 23; 2 Samuel 9:7,13 — The table of the King; eating at the King's table. • Luke 22:20 — "This cup is the new covenant in My blood." • John 1:12 — Children of God by receiving and believing. • John 3:18 — Outside of Christ, judgment remains. • Matthew 28:19–20 — The Great Commission. • Romans 8:1 — No condemnation in Christ Jesus. • Romans 8:17 — Heirs of God and co-heirs with Christ. • Romans 10:9 — Confess and believe: salvation. • 2 Corinthians 5:17, 21 — New creation; righteousness of God in Christ. • 2 Corinthians 12:10 — When I am weak, then I am strong. • Ephesians 1:4–6 — Chosen and adopted in love. • Ephesians 2:6 — Seated with Christ in the heavenly realms. • Colossians 1:13 — Delivered from the domain of darkness. • 1 Peter 2:9 — A chosen people, a royal priesthood. • Hebrews 9:16–17 — A testament (will) is in force through death. • Hebrews 10:14 — Perfected forever by one sacrifice. • 2 Timothy 2:13 — He remains faithful. • Ezekiel 18:20 — The soul who sins shall die; no generational guilt. • Revelation 19:9 — Blessed are those invited to the marriage supper of the Lamb. • 1 Peter 5:8 — The adversary prowls like a roaring lion.

About the Author

Cole Bradshaw is the founder of The FaithFull Marriage, a ministry devoted to proclaiming the gospel of Jesus Christ, teaching biblical covenant, and helping couples and churches walk in Christ-centered faithfulness. Rescued from performance-driven religion into the freedom of covenant grace, Cole writes and speaks to call people out of Lo-Debar and into the Father's table.

Together with his wife, Zaily, Cole creates resources, studies, and gatherings that equip believers to live out the gospel in everyday life. They serve the local church in Utah and love seeing lives transformed by the kindness of the King—given to us for Jesus' sake.

Contact: thefaithfullmarriage@gmail.com YouTube: @faithfullmarriage

Scripture References

1 Samuel 18:3–4, 1 Samuel 20:14–15, 1 Samuel 31:1–6, 2 Samuel 4:4, 2 Samuel 9:1–13, 2 Samuel 21:1, 7–8, Psalm 23, Luke 22:20, John 1:12, John 3:18, Matthew 28:19–20, Romans 8:1, Romans 8:17, Romans 10:9, 2 Corinthians 5:17, 21, 2 Corinthians 12:10, Ephesians 1:4–6, Ephesians 2:6, Colossians 1:13, 1 Peter 2:9, Hebrews 9:16–17, Hebrews 10:14, 2 Timothy 2:13, Ezekiel 18:20, Revelation 19:9, 1 Peter 5:8

Invitation & Resources

The covenant has already been cut. The blood of Jesus has sealed it. The Father is inviting you to take your seat at His table today. If you confess with your mouth, "Jesus is Lord," and believe in your heart that God raised Him from the dead, you will be saved (Romans 10:9).

If you or your church ever need encouragement in your marriage journey, we'd love to come alongside you as friends who understand the real struggles and joys of covenant life. You don't have to walk it alone.

We've created resources through our ministry, The FaithFull Marriage, including:

• The FaithFull Marriage workbook — designed for couples to grow deeper in Christ and with each other.

• FaithFull Pre-Marriage workbook — written to help couples prepare for covenant life together.

These workbooks are being used in small group studies, one-on-one mentoring, and counseling settings, and they can be a great resource for your family or church.

You can connect with us here:

■ faithfullmarriage@gmail.com

■ YouTube: @faithfullmarriage

Notes

Notes

Notes

Notes

Notes

Notes

Notes

Notes

Notes

Notes

Notes

Notes

Notes

Notes

Notes

Made in the USA
Coppell, TX
16 January 2026

69206136R00028